Contents

Image credits

Cover and Title page © Vectomart*, p5 Solar System ©NASA/JPL, p6 Main picture ©peresanz*, p6 Milky Way illustration ©Vividfour*, p8 Eros ©NASA/Goddard Space Flight Center Scientific Visualization Studio, p9 Hale-Bopp comet ©NASA, p9 Meteroid ©max voran*, p9 Comet ©N/A*, p11 Sun ©xfox01*, p11 Jupiter ©NASA/JPL/University of Arizona, p11 Earth ©NASA, p12 Milky Way illustration ©Vividfour*, p12 Sunspot image ©John R Smith*, p13 Earth ©NASA, p13 Solar flare ©NASA, p14 Mercury ©NASA/Johns Hopkins University Applied Physics Laboratory/Carnegie Institution of Washington, p14 Venus ©NASA/JPL, p15 Earth ©NASA, p15 Mars ©NASA/JPL, p15 Ceres ©NASA, p17 Mercury ©Luis Stortini Sabor aka CVADRAT*, p17 Earth ©NASA, p19 Mercury ©Luis Stortini Sabor aka CVADRAT*, p19 Mercury transit ©Phil Jones, p19 Mercury statue ©Oleg Golovnev*, p21 Venus ©NASA/JPL, p21 Earth ©NASA, p22 Venus clouds ©NASA, p23 Sun ©xfox01*, p24 Earth ©NASA, p24 Venus ©NASA/JPL, p24 Gula Mons ©NASA/JPL, p25 Earth ©NASA, p27 Mt Etna ©Fredy Thuerig*, p28 Earth ©NASA, p28 Sun ©xfox01*, p29 Tilted Earth ©NASA, p29 Earth ©NASA, p29 Atmosphere ©NASA/JPL/UCSD/JSC, p29 Sun ©xfox01*, p30 Lunar eclipse ©Primo_ Cigler*, p30 Solar eclipse ©Vladimir Wrangel*, p30 Tilted Earth ©NASA, p30 Moon ©Lick Observatory, p31 Moon ©Lick Observatory, p31 Earth ©NASA, p33 Mars ©NASA/JPL, p33 Earth ©NASA, p34 Martian landscape top ©NASA/JPL-Caltech/ University of Arizona, p34 Martian landscape bottom ©Malin Space Science Systems/ NASA, p35 Phobos ©G. Neukum/NASA, p35 Mars surface ©NASA/JPL, p36 Asteroid shapes and sizes ©NASA/JPL-Caltech/JAXA/ESA, p37 Ida nine views ©NASA/USGS, p38 Jupiter ©NASA/JPL/University of Arizona, p39 Saturn ©George Toubalis*, p39 Uranus ©NASA/Space Telescope Science Institute, p39 Neptune ©NASA, p41 Jupiter ©NASA/JPL/University of Arizona, p41 Earth ©NASA, p42 Io volcanoes etc ©NASA/ JPL, p43 Jupiter and moons ©Jan Sandberg Wikipedia, p43 Galilean moons ©NASA/ JPL-Caltech Wikipedia, p43 Thebe ©NASA/JPL Wikipedia, p44 Jupiter interior ©G. Neukum/NASA, p44 Jupiter ©NASA/JPL/University of Arizona, p45 Earth ©NASA, p45 Great Red Spot ©NASA/JPL, p46 Saturn ©George Toubalis*, p47 Earth ©NASA, p48 Saturns rings tilt ©NASA and The Hubble Heritage Team, p49 Coloured rings ©NASA, p49 Saturn edge on ©Erich Karkoschka (University of Arizona Lunar & Planetary Lab) and NASA, p50 Titan behind rings ©NASA/JPL/Space Science Institute, p51 Saturn's moons Wikipedia Commons, p52 Saturn storm ©NASA/JPL, p53 Earth ©NASA, p53 Jupiter ©NASA/JPL/University of Arizona, p53 Saturn ©George Toubalis*, p53 Saturn from above ©GI0ck*, p55 Uranus ©NASA/Space Telescope Science Institute, p56 Uranus moons Wikipedia Commons, p57 Miranda ©NASA/JPL, p58 Neptune ©NASA, p59 Earth ©NASA, p60 Neptune clouds ©NASA Jet Propulsion Laboratory, p61 Triton ©NASA/JPL, p61 Neptune Great Dark Spot ©NASA, p61 Sun ©xfox01*, p61 Earth ©NASA, p61 Neptune ©NASA, p63 Pluto ©NASA, p63 Earth ©NASA, p64 Pluto & Charon ©NASA/JPL, p65 Pluto ©NASA, p66 Parts of a comet ©Mark R*, p67 Tempel 1 ©NASA/JPL-Caltech/UMD Wikipedia, p67 Comet McNaught ©European Southern Observatory/NASA, p67 Comet ©N/A*, p68 Sputnik 1 ©NSSDC, NASA Wikipedia, p68 Astronaut ©NASA, p68 Mars Rover ©NASA, p69 Hubble Telescope ©NASA Wikipedia, p69 Space Shuttle ©NASA, p69 Voyager 2 ©NASA/ JPL, p69 Apollo 11 ©NASA, p70 Sun ©xfox01*, p70 Mercury ©Luis Stortini Sabor aka CVADRAT*, p70 Venus ©NASA/JPL, p71 Earth ©NASA, p71 Mars ©NASA/JPL, p71 Jupiter ©NASA/JPL/University of Arizona, p71 Saturn ©George Toubalis*, p71 Uranus ©NASA/Space Telescope Science Institute, p71 Neptune ©NASA, p71 Pluto ©NASA, p72 Jupiter ©NASA/JPL/University of Arizona, p72/73 Jupiter moons Jan Sandberg Wikipedia, p73 Earth ©NASA, p73 Moon ©Lick Observatory/NASA.

*Images from Shutterstock.com

Introduction

Our Solar System is a busy place, consisting of eight planets, dwarf planets, moons, asteroids, meteoroids, comets, ice and huge amounts of dust and gas that are all travelling around the Sun. *Solar* is a Latin term meaning Sun, and it is this large yellow star that plays an important role in the middle of our Solar System. Due to its size (it contains over 98 per cent of the entire mass of the Solar System), the Sun has a very powerful gravitational pull, attracting all the other planets towards it.

Astronomers have studied the Solar System for thousands of years and are still making new discoveries. The larger, more complex objects that have been discovered are the planets and they all have different characteristics.

There are four inner planets: Mercury, Venus, Earth and Mars. They are said to be terrestrial, in that they are composed mainly of rock, are relatively small, and have few or no moons.

The outer planets include: Jupiter, Saturn, Uranus and Neptune. They are called the Jovian planets. They are large and made up of gas, are ringed, and have many moons.

Pluto was reclassified from a planet to a dwarf planet in 2006. It is actually more like a comet than a planet, with one large moon and three small moons.

The Milky Way

The Milky Way is the name of the
spiral galaxy in which our Solar System
is located. All the stars that we see
in the night sky are part of the Milky
Way galaxy. Aside from the relatively
nearby stars, the galaxy appears as
a hazy band of white light. The Solar
System is located in the Milky Way
halfway out from the centre.

The Solar System

The Milky Way

The Solar System

The Solar System is the Sun and the many objects that orbit it. These objects include eight planets, at least five dwarf planets and countless asteroids, meteoroids and comets. Orbiting some of the planets and dwarf planets are over 160 moons. The Sun keeps its surrounding objects in its orbit by its pull of gravity which has an influence for many millions of kilometres.

Eros – an asteroid

Saturn

Asteroid Belt

Jupiter

Sun

Mars

Earth

Venus

Mercury

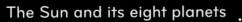

The Sun and its eight planets

A meteoroid enters the Earth's atmosphere

Neptune

Uranus

Comet

The Sun

Our star

The Sun is the star of our Solar System. It is a huge ball of scorching hot glowing gases. Heat and light from this star travel millions of kilometres to reach Earth and support all life on our planet. The Sun is large enough to contain every single other object in the Solar System. It is almost ten times wider than the next largest object in the Solar System, which is Jupiter.

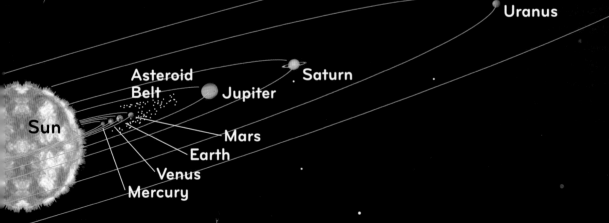

Sun

Mercury

Venus

Earth

Mars

Asteroid Belt

Jupiter

Saturn

Uranus

Neptune

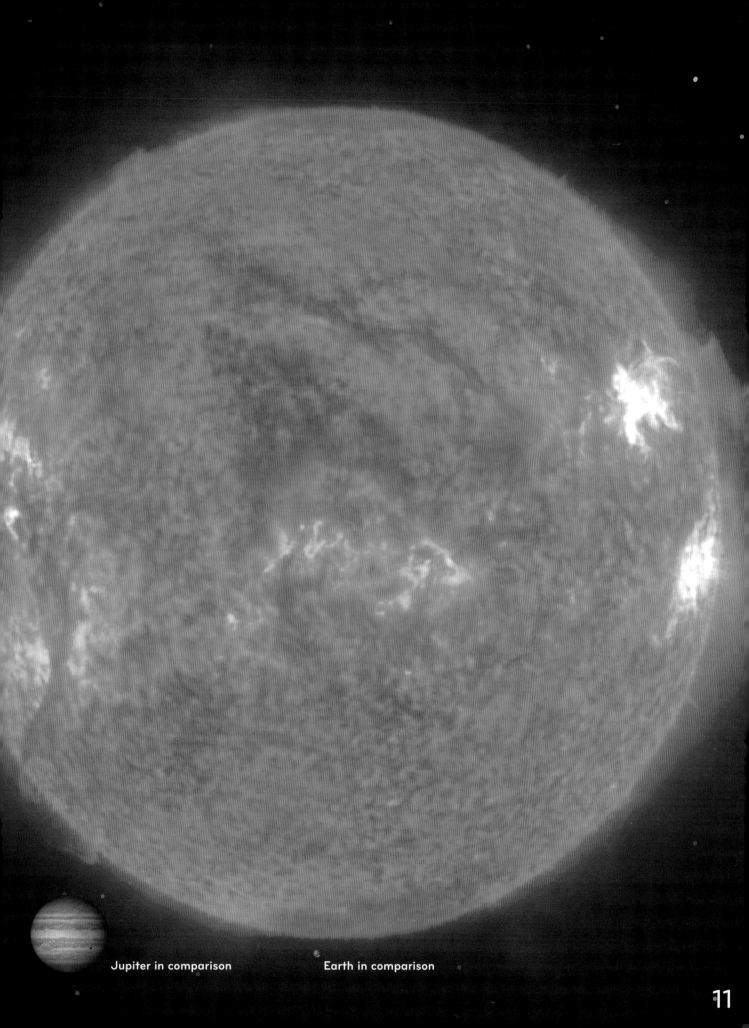

Jupiter in comparison   Earth in comparison

The Sun Facts

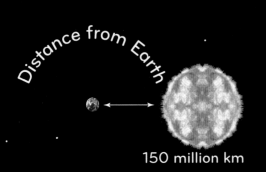

Distance from Earth
150 million km

Length of galactic year
230 million Earth years

Length of day
25 Earth days 9 hours

Diameter
1 391 016 km

Circumference
4 370 000 km

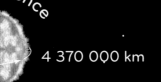

Average temperature
5504 °C

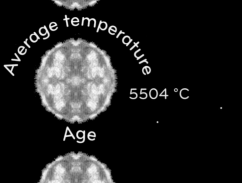

Age
4.6 billion years

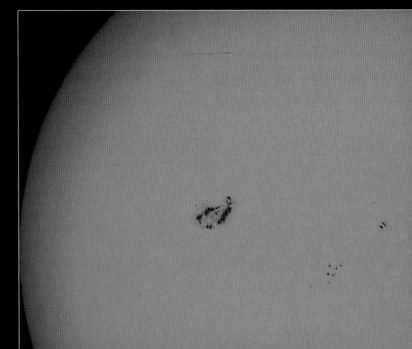

Sunspots are relatively cool, dark patches on the Sun's surface. They come in many shapes and sizes and often appear in groups. Sunspots can be over ten times the diameter of Earth.

Earth in comparison

A massive solar flare erupts from the Sun's surface

Inner Solar System

There are four inner planets: Mercury, Venus, Earth and Mars. They are closest to the Sun and are known as the terrestrial planets because their surfaces are solid and rocky. The four planets are very different from each other and their surfaces are dotted with impact craters, valleys and some volcanoes. The Asteroid Belt is a region beyond the orbit of Mars where thousands of asteroids are found orbiting the Sun.

Mercury
The smallest planet in the Inner Solar System

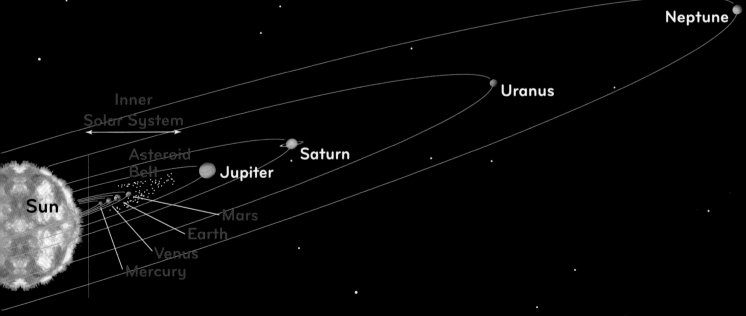

Neptune

Uranus

Inner
Solar System

Saturn

Asteroid
Belt

Jupiter

Mars

Earth

Venus

Mercury

Sun

Venus
Clouds of sulphuric acid prevent its surface being seen from Earth

Earth
The only planet in the Solar System known to have life

Ceres
The largest object in the Asteroid Belt

Mars
Named after the Roman god of war, it is often described as the "Red Planet"

Mercury
The closest planet to the Sun

Mercury is the smallest planet. It is closest to the Sun and takes only eighty-eight Earth days to complete an orbit of the Sun. Mercury is scorching hot on its sunlit side, however it has no atmosphere to retain this heat so temperatures on its unlit side are extremely cold.

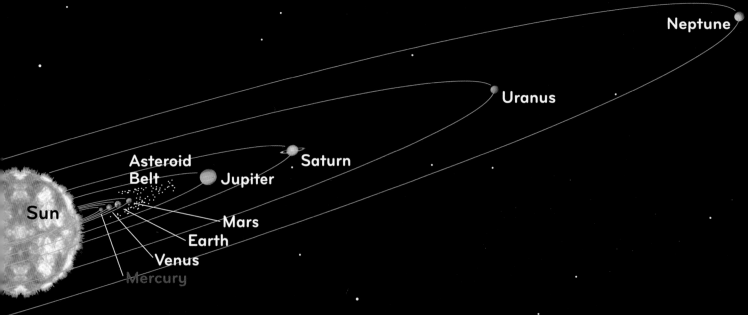

Neptune

Uranus

Saturn

Asteroid
Belt

Jupiter

Sun

Mars

Earth

Venus

Mercury

16

Cratered surface is evidence of
many asteroid and meteor impacts

Mercury and Earth compared

Mercury Facts

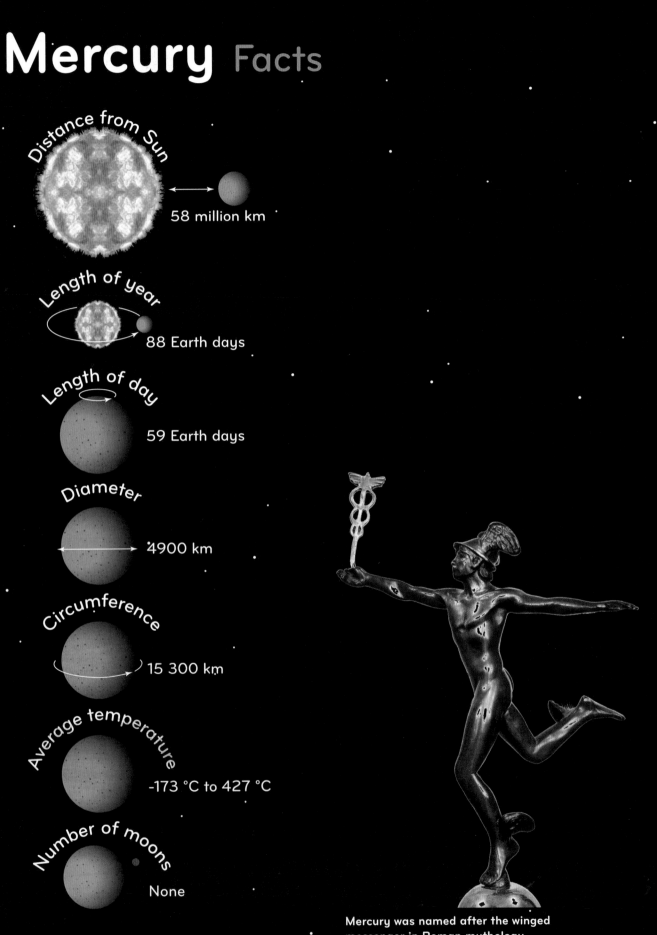

Distance from Sun

58 million km

Length of year

88 Earth days

Length of day

59 Earth days

Diameter

4900 km

Circumference

15 300 km

Average temperature

-173 °C to 427 °C

Number of moons

None

Mercury was named after the winged messenger in Roman mythology

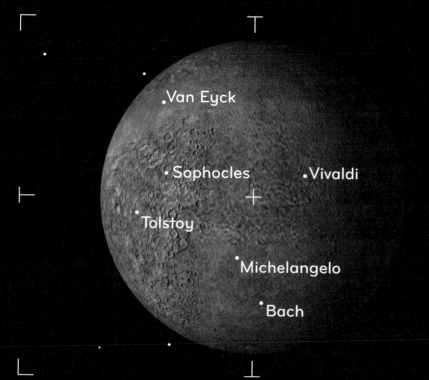

Van Eyck

Sophocles

Vivaldi

Tolstoy

Michelangelo

Bach

Many of the craters on Mercury have been named after famous writers, musicians, painters and other artists

This small black dot is Mercury passing in front of the Sun when seen from Earth

Venus
Earth's neighbour

Venus is named after the Roman goddess of love and beauty because of its brightness and beauty in the night sky. It is the brightest object in the sky after the Sun and Earth's moon. It is the second planet from the Sun in the Solar System and the nearest planet to Earth. Venus is covered by a thick rapidly swirling atmosphere and temperatures are the hottest on any planet in the Solar System. The surface is covered by gently rolling hills and lava flows. There are not many mountains.

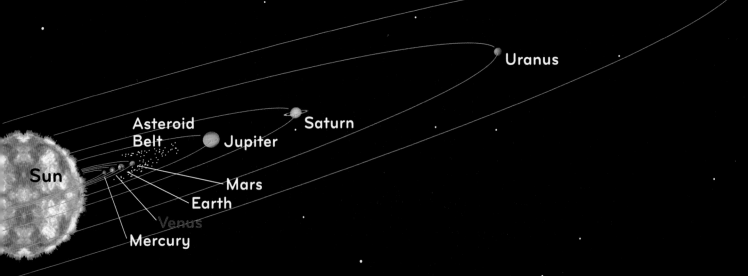

Neptune

Uranus

Asteroid
Belt

Saturn

Jupiter

Sun

Mars

Earth

Venus

Mercury

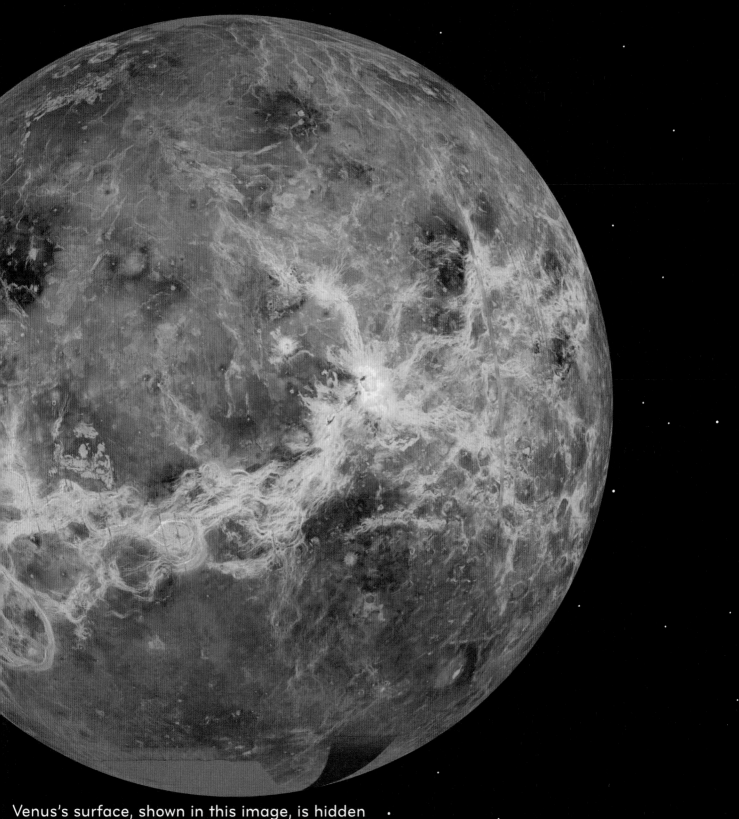

Venus's surface, shown in this image, is hidden
by dense clouds that contain sulphuric acid

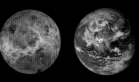

Venus and Earth compared

Venus Facts

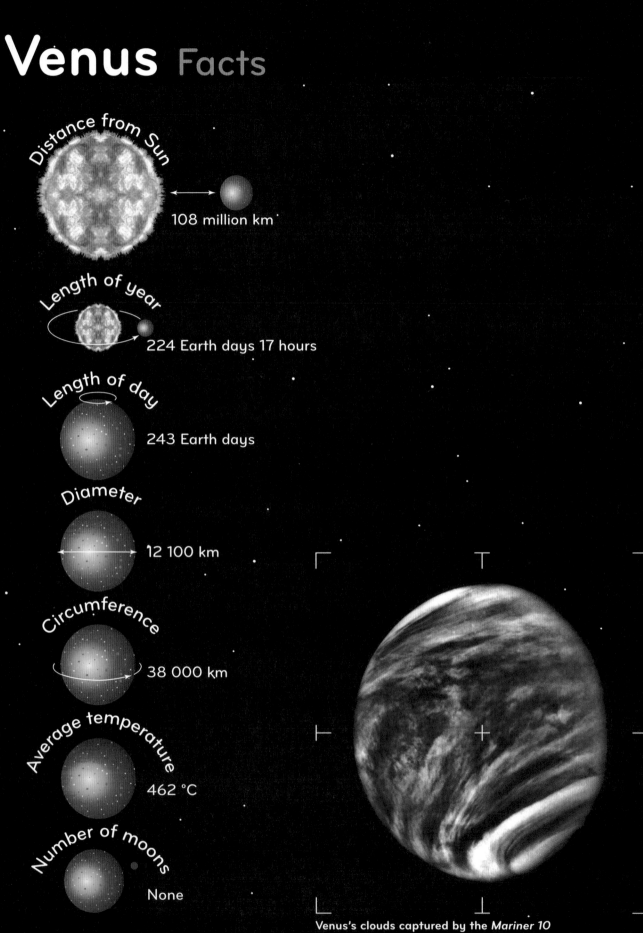

Distance from Sun
108 million km

Length of year
224 Earth days 17 hours

Length of day
243 Earth days

Diameter
12 100 km

Circumference
38 000 km

Average temperature
462 °C

Number of moons
None

Venus's clouds captured by the *Mariner 10* spacecraft in early 1974

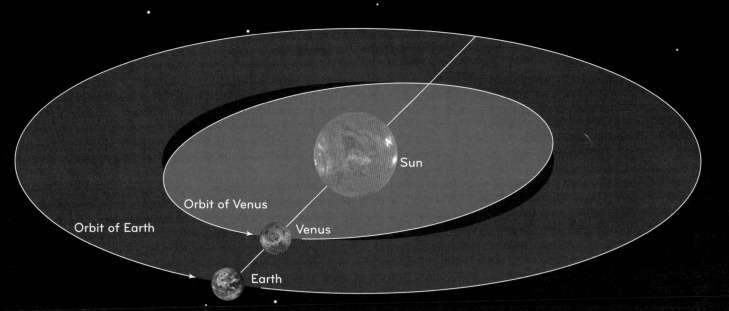

Orbit of Venus

Orbit of Earth

Sun

Venus

Earth

Venus's orbit is tilted in respect to the orbit of Earth

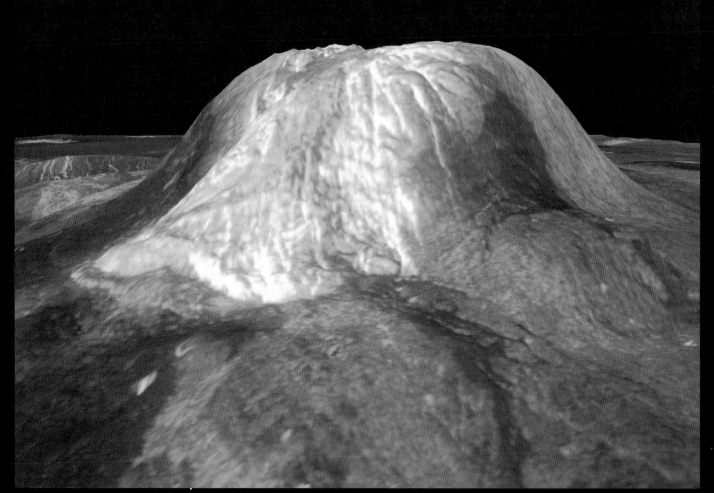

Gula Mons is a 3 km high volcano on the surface of Venus

Earth
Our home in space

Earth is the only planet in the Universe known to support life! It is a living planet, with plently of water, trees, plants and breathable air, protected by its atmosphere. It is the third planet from the Sun and is largest of the four rocky inner planets. Oceans, at least 4 kilometres deep, cover nearly 70 per cent of Earth's surface. It has one moon which is the only other place to be visited by people from Earth. It takes Earth 365 days and 6 hours (one year) to orbit the Sun.

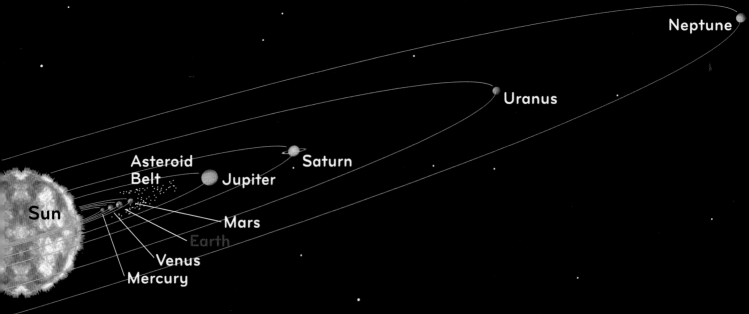

Neptune

Uranus

Saturn

Asteroid
Belt

Jupiter

Sun

Mars

Earth

Venus

Mercury

Earth is the third planet from the Sun and is home
to millions of species, including humans

main layers called the crust, mantle, and core. The crust, the outermost layer, is rigid and very thin compared with the other two. Beneath the oceans, the crust varies little in thickness, generally extending only to about 5 kilometres. The thickness of the crust beneath continents is much more variable but averages at about 30 kilometres and under large mountain ranges, such as the Alps or the Sierra Nevada, the base of the crust can be as deep as 100 kilometres. The Earth's crust is brittle and can break. It is made up of separate pieces called plates. These are always moving and earthquakes often occur at the points where they meet.

hot layer of semi-solid rock approximately 2900 kilometres thick. At the centre of the Earth lies the core, the inner part of which is solid.

The structure of Earth

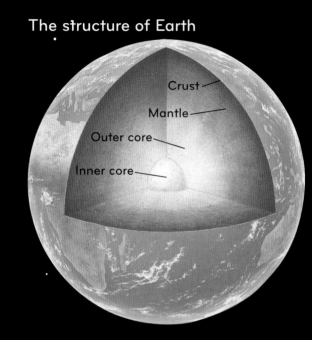

Crust
Mantle
Outer core
Inner core

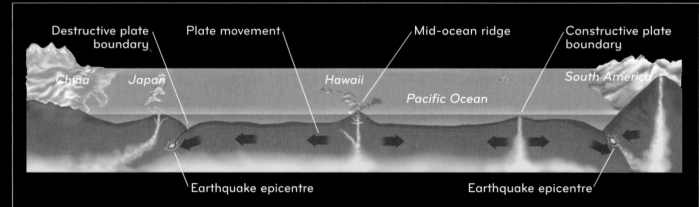

Destructive plate boundary
Plate movement
Mid-ocean ridge
Constructive plate boundary

China   Japan   Hawaii   South America

Pacific Ocean

Earthquake epicentre   Earthquake epicentre

A cross-section through the Pacific Ocean showing the plate structure

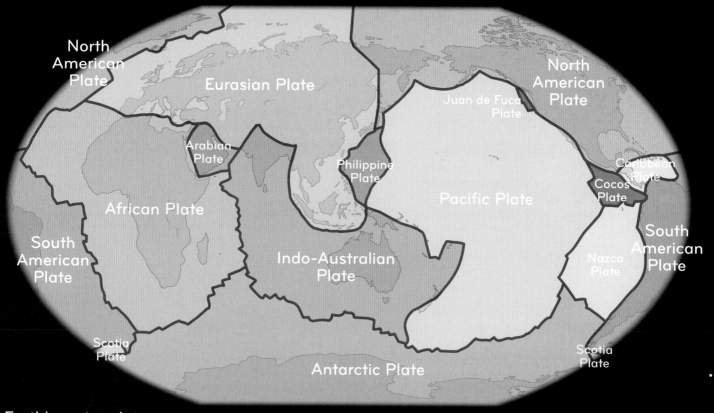

North
American
Plate

Eurasian Plate

North
American
Plate

Juan de Fuca
Plate

Arabian
Plate

Philippine
Plate

Caribbean
Plate

Cocos
Plate

Pacific Plate

African Plate

South
American
Plate

Indo-Australian
Plate

Nazca
Plate

South
American
Plate

Scotia
Plate

Antarctic Plate

Scotia
Plate

Earth's major plates

Mt Etna on Sicily, Italy

Loss of life in the ten most deadly earthquakes since 1900

Year	Location	Deaths
1976	China	255 000
2004	Indonesia/Indian Ocean	225 000
2010	Haiti	222 570
1920	China	200 000
1927	China	200 000
1923	Japan	142 807
1908	Italy	110 000
2005	Pakistan	74 648
1932	China	70 000
1970	Peru	66 794

Earth Facts

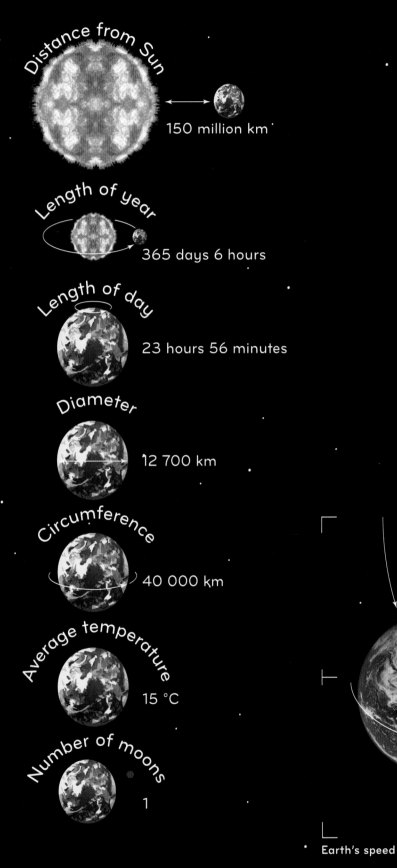

Distance from Sun

150 million km

Length of year

365 days 6 hours

Length of day

23 hours 56 minutes

Diameter

12 700 km

Circumference

40 000 km

Average temperature

15 °C

Number of moons

1

Earth moves around the Sun at 108 000 kilometres / hour

At the equator Earth rotates at 1670 kilometres / hour

Earth's speed

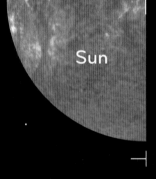

Sun

The effect of Earth's tilt

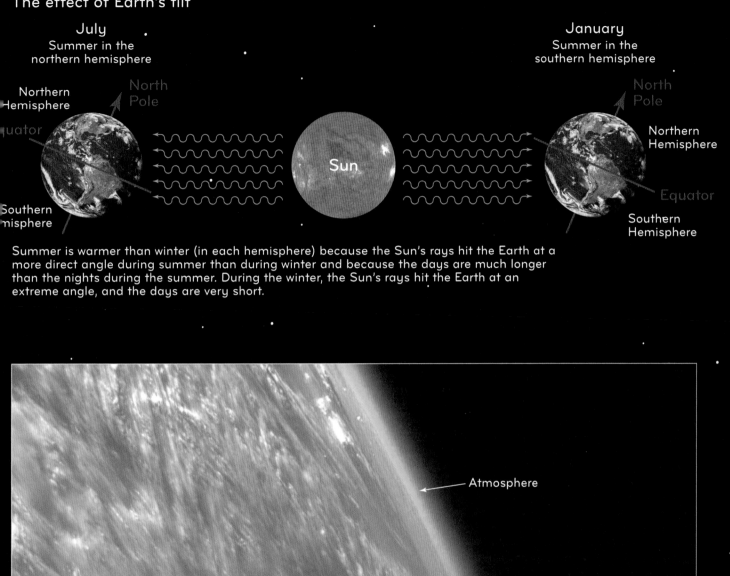

July — Summer in the northern hemisphere

North Pole
Northern Hemisphere
Equator
Southern Hemisphere

Sun

January — Summer in the southern hemisphere

North Pole
Northern Hemisphere
Equator
Southern Hemisphere

Summer is warmer than winter (in each hemisphere) because the Sun's rays hit the Earth at a more direct angle during summer than during winter and because the days are much longer than the nights during the summer. During the winter, the Sun's rays hit the Earth at an extreme angle, and the days are very short.

— Atmosphere

Earth's atmosphere is about 450 km thick

Earth's companion

The Moon

The Moon is Earth's only natural satellite. It is the second brightest object in the sky after the Sun and is thought to have formed from the debris when a planet-sized object collided with Earth billions of years ago. It is the only object, other than Earth, to have been stepped on by human beings. Its Roman name is *Luna* and its Greek name is *Selene*. Although the Moon's appearance changes due to its phases, you are only ever able to see one side of it as it always faces Earth.

There are a lot of dark patches on the moon which are flat areas of old lava flows which look like seas. The surface is very mountainous and there are peaks nearly as high as Mount Everest (the highest mountain on Earth).

The Moon's orbital plane is inclined in relation to the Earth's

Moon's orbit

Earth's orbit

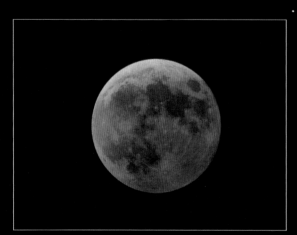

A lunar eclipse occurs when the Earth passes between the Sun and Moon

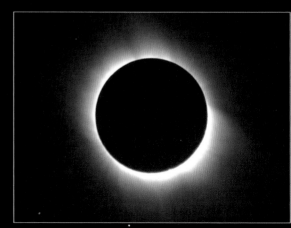

A solar eclipse occurs when the Moon passes between the Sun and Earth

The phases of the Moon

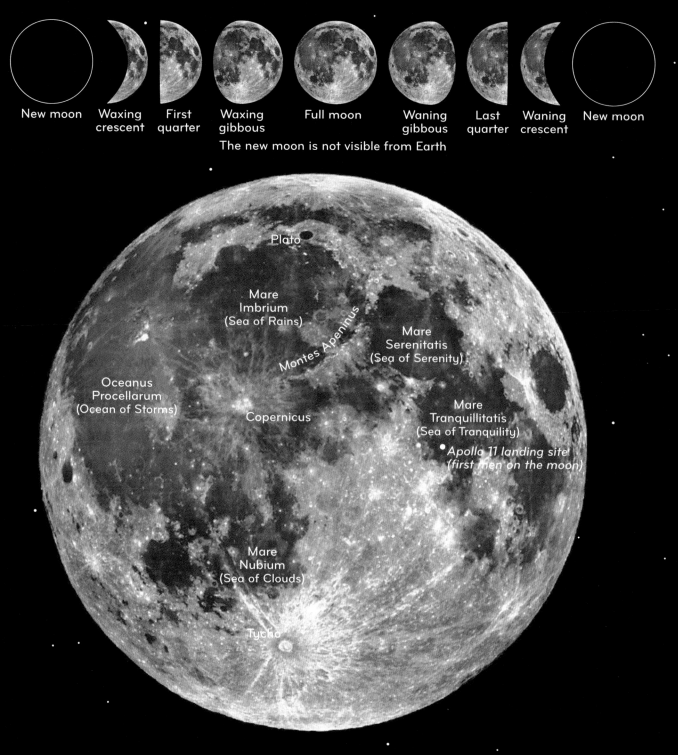

New moon   Waxing crescent   First quarter   Waxing gibbous   Full moon   Waning gibbous   Last quarter   Waning crescent   New moon

The new moon is not visible from Earth

Plato

Mare Imbrium
(Sea of Rains)

Montes Apeninus

Mare Serenitatis
(Sea of Serenity)

Oceanus Procellarum
(Ocean of Storms)

Copernicus

Mare Tranquillitatis
(Sea of Tranquility)

*Apollo 11 landing site
(first men on the moon)*

Mare Nubium
(Sea of Clouds)

Tycho

Only one side of the Moon is visible from Earth, the far side has only been seen by the few astronauts whose spaceships orbited it in the late 1960s and early 1970s.

The Moon and Earth compared

Mars
The red planet

Mars is the fourth planet from the Sun and because of its blood red colour has been named after the Roman god of war. Its surface has been affected by volcanoes, crustal movements and dust storms. Mars has the tallest mountain in the Solar System, Olympus Mons, which rises 24 kilometres above the surrounding land.

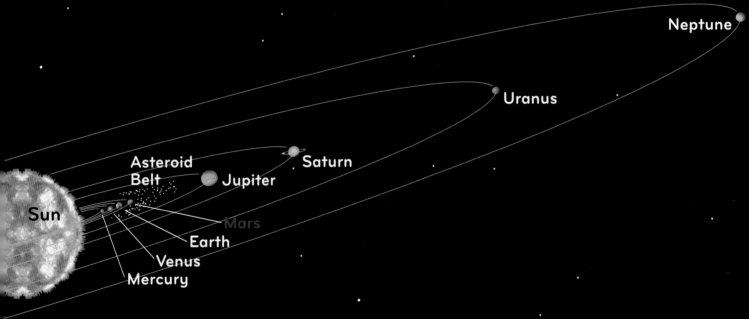

Neptune

Uranus

Saturn

Asteroid
Belt

Jupiter

Sun

Mars

Earth

Venus

Mercury

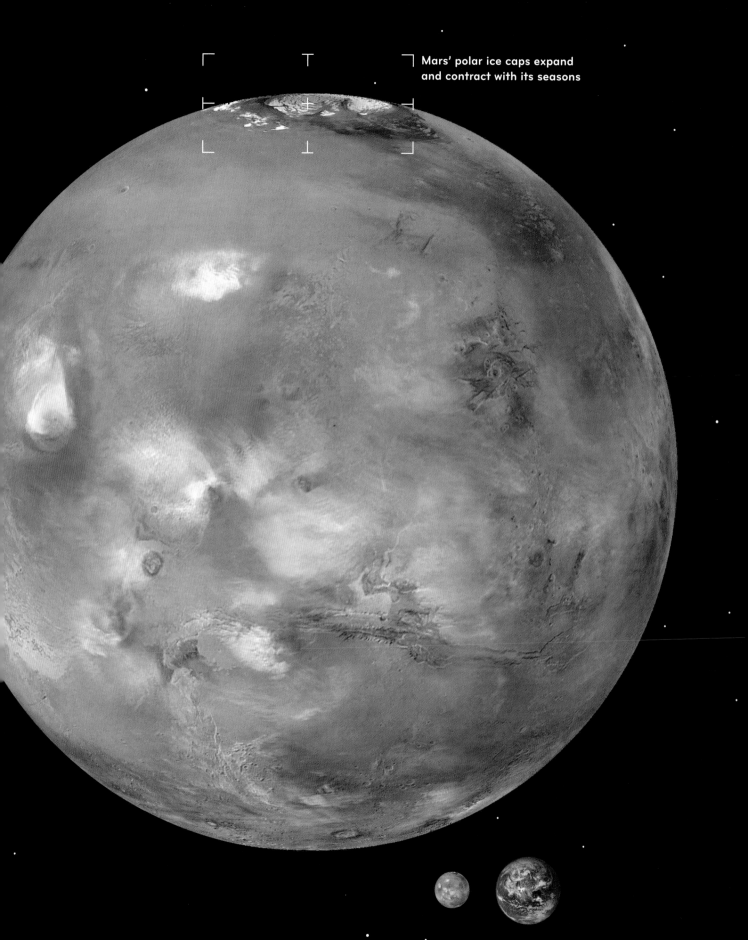

Mars' polar ice caps expand
and contract with its seasons

Mars and Earth compared

33

Mars Facts

Distance from Sun

228 million km

Length of year

687 Earth days

Length of day

24 hours 37 minutes

Diameter

6779 km

Circumference

21 300 km

Average temperature

-63 °C

Number of moons

2

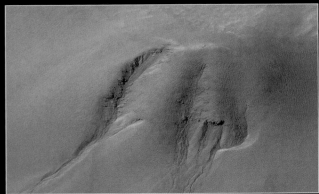

Martian landscapes

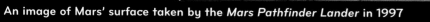

Phobos, the larger of Mars' two tiny moons, is only 27 km across

An image of Mars' surface taken by the *Mars Pathfinder Lander* in 1997

Asteroids

Asteroids are small lumps of rocks and ice which orbit the Sun like mini-planets. There are millions of asteroids, and like most other small bodies, asteroids are often thought to be the shattered remnants of objects within the young Solar System that never grew large enough to become planets.

Asteroids come in many shapes and sizes

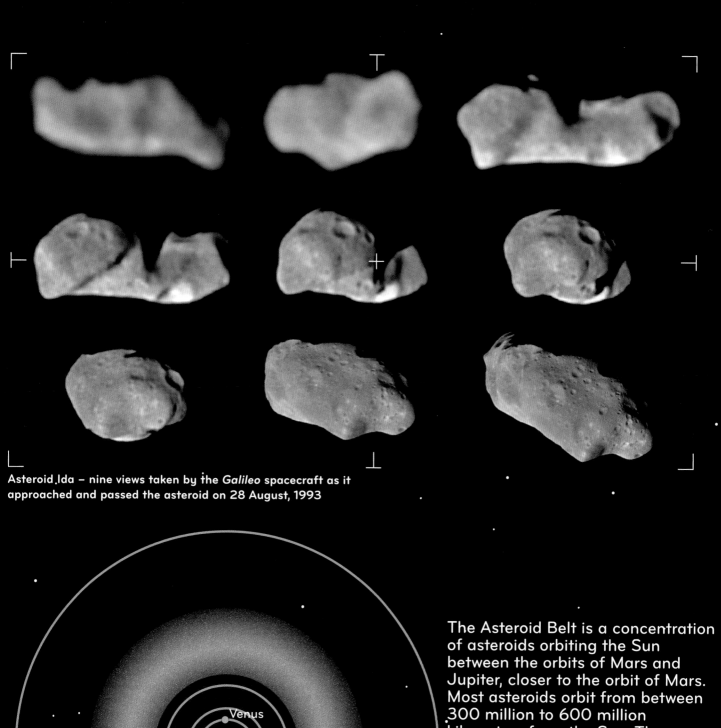

Asteroid Ida – nine views taken by the *Galileo* spacecraft as it approached and passed the asteroid on 28 August, 1993

The Asteroid Belt is a concentration of asteroids orbiting the Sun between the orbits of Mars and Jupiter, closer to the orbit of Mars. Most asteroids orbit from between 300 million to 600 million kilometres from the Sun. The asteroids in the Asteroid Belt have slightly elliptical orbits. The time for one revolution around the Sun varies from about three to six Earth years.

Outer Solar System

The outer planets are: Jupiter, Saturn, Uranus and Neptune. They are sometimes known as the Gas Giants as they are huge in comparison to the inner planets and, made up mostly of gas, do not have solid surfaces. All four have rings around them, with Saturn's being the most famous. The four planets also have large numbers of moons orbiting them.

Neptune

Uranus

Saturn

Asteroid
Belt

Jupiter

Sun

Mars

Earth

Venus

Mercury

Outer
Solar System

Jupiter
The fifth planet from the Sun
and the largest planet

Saturn
The rings of Saturn may be less
than 10 metres thick in places

Uranus
Uranus was the
first planet discovered
with a telescope

Neptune
Named for the Roman
god of the sea, it is the
fourth-largest planet

Jupiter
The giant planet

Jupiter is the largest planet in the Solar System. It is more than 300 times bigger than Earth. The planet is the fourth brightest object visible from Earth after the Sun, the Earth's moon and Venus. Its main feature is a Great Red Spot, which is a storm that has been going on for years. Jupiter has a ring system like all of the large gas planets, although these rings are not as famous or as visible as Saturn's. Orbiting Jupiter are at least sixty-three moons.

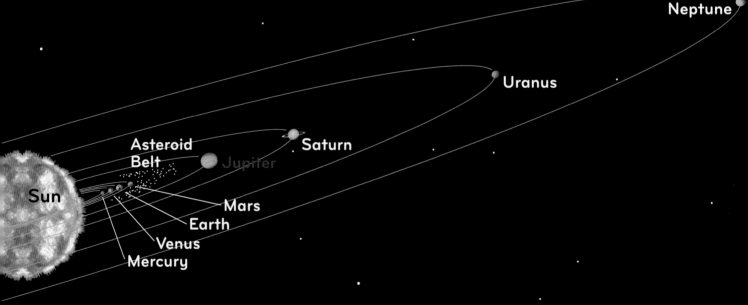

Neptune

Uranus

Saturn

Asteroid
Belt

Jupiter

Sun

Mars

Earth

Venus

Mercury

Great Red Spot

Shadow of one
of Jupiter's moons

Earth in comparison

Jupiter's moons

The Sun is a star with eight planets orbiting it. Jupiter also seems to have its very own solar system with at least sixty-three very different moons orbiting it. Most of these moons are very small and are probably asteroids caught by Jupiter's strong gravitational pull to remain in orbit around the planet. The four largest moons, Io, Europa, Ganymede and Callisto are like little worlds, each different from each other. They are known as the Galilean satellites and can be seen with the aid of binoculars.

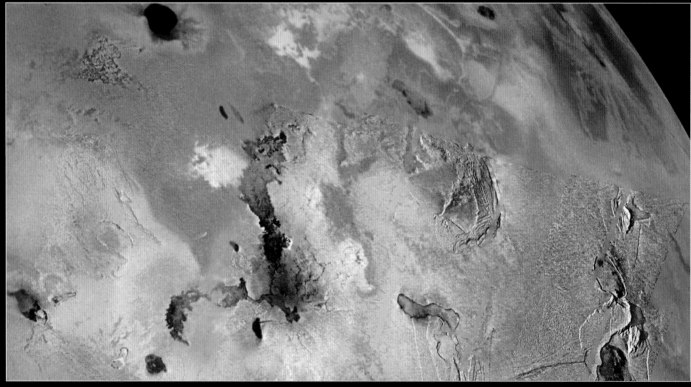

An image of the mountains and volcanoes on Io taken by the *Galileo* spacecraft in 1999

Jupiter and the four moons discovered in 1610 by Galileo Galilei

Io, with over 400 active volcanoes, is the most geologically active object in the Solar System

Ganymede is the largest moon in the Solar System and is larger than the planet Mercury.

Europa is the smallest of the Galilean moons and orbits Jupiter in just over three and a half days

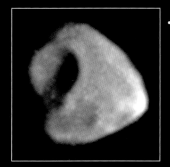

Thebe, one of Jupiter's smallest moons, is about 100 km across and takes just over 16 hours to orbit Jupiter

Callisto has one of the most heavily cratered surfaces in the Solar System

43

Jupiter Facts

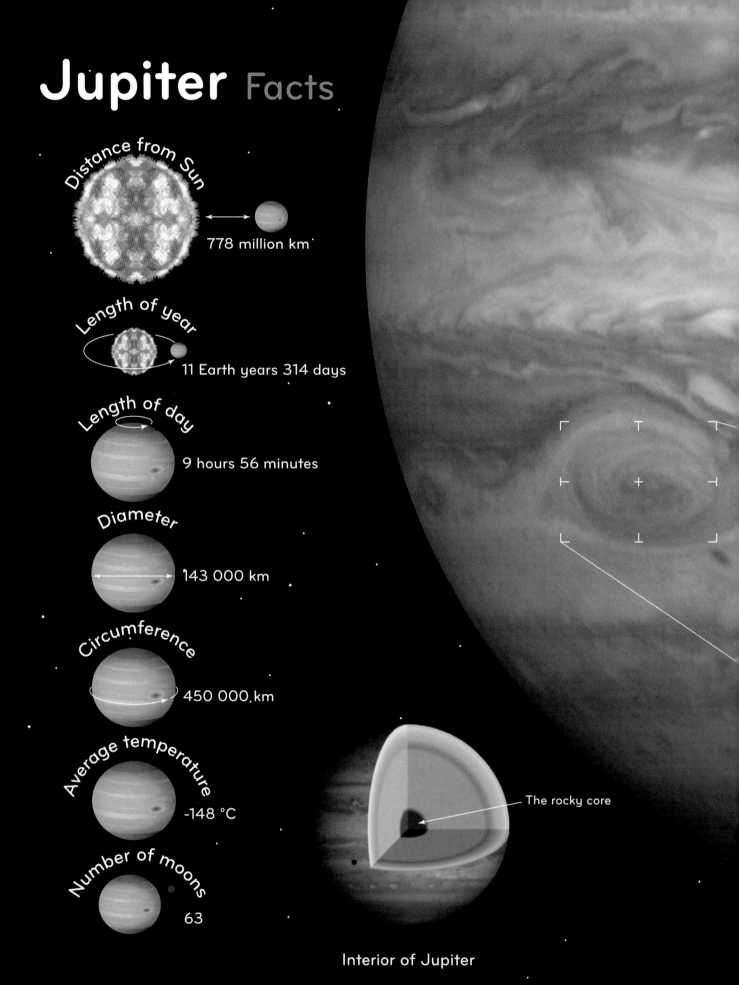

Distance from Sun
778 million km

Length of year
11 Earth years 314 days

Length of day
9 hours 56 minutes

Diameter
143 000 km

Circumference
450 000 km

Average temperature
-148 °C

Number of moons
63

The rocky core

Interior of Jupiter

Saturn

The ringed planet

Saturn is the second largest planet in the Solar System. It is often called the ringed planet because it is surrounded by rings of dust and rocks. Like Jupiter Saturn is a gas giant and is made up mainly of hydrogen. It is very light and if placed in a big pond of water it would float. Saturn spins very quickly. It takes only ten hours to rotate fully. A year on Saturn would take almost thirty Earth years. However, a day on Saturn is about ten and a half hours.

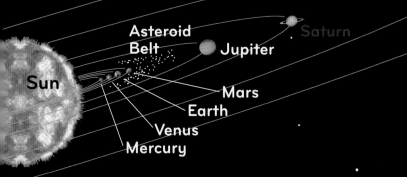

Neptune

Uranus

Saturn

Asteroid
Belt

Jupiter

Sun

Mars

Earth

Venus

Mercury

Saturn's rings are one of the most spectacular
and beautiful sights in the Solar System

Earth in comparison

Saturn's rings

Saturn's rings are probably the most distinguishing feature of any planet in the Solar System. The width of the planet is 116 500 kilometres, but the rings surrounding it increase this width to around 270 000 kilometres. The rings are about one kilometre thick and are made up of particles ranging in size from specks of dust to massive icy boulders.

Saturn's rings slowly tilt when viewed from Earth, as this sequence taken from 1996–2000 shows

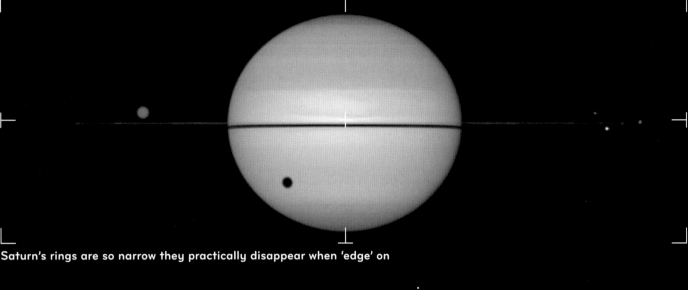

Saturn's rings are so narrow they practically disappear when 'edge' on

Saturn's rings are divided into eight major ring divisions.
Each ring orbits at a different speed around the planet

Saturn's moons

Orbiting Saturn are at least sixty-two moons. Most of these moons are quite small. However, 1 221 860 kilometres away from Saturn is the second biggest moon in the Solar System: Titan. Titan is an extremely interesting moon. It is the only moon in the Solar System to have an atmosphere which is made up mainly of nitrogen. Some hydrocarbons present in Titan's atmosphere make it appear an orange colour.

This image shows the giant moon Titan behind
Saturn's rings and the tiny moon Epimetheus

Hyperion is the largest
irregularly shaped
moon ever observed

Mimas has a large
crater almost one-third
of its diameter

Iapetus has a
mountain ridge
over 20 km high

Pheobe orbits Saturn in
the opposite direction to
most other moons

Rhea is Saturn's
second-largest moon

Titan is Saturn's largest moon
and the second-largest in the
Solar System

Saturn Facts

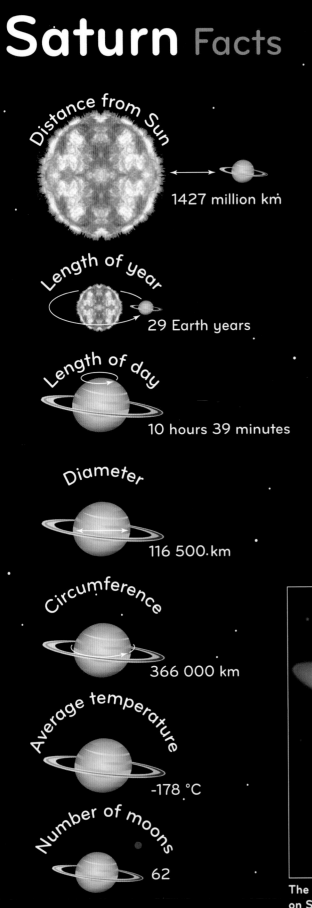

Distance from Sun
1427 million km

Length of year
29 Earth years

Length of day
10 hours 39 minutes

Diameter
116 500 km

Circumference
366 000 km

Average temperature
-178 °C

Number of moons
62

The bright feature on this image is a storm
on Saturn's surface with an estimated speed
of over 1500 km per hour

Saturn is more than twice the distance away from Earth as Jupiter

Earth

Jupiter

Saturn

629 million km

1277 million km

116 500 km

270 000 km

Saturn's rings are more than twice the planet's diameter

Uranus

The blue planet

Uranus was first identified as a planet in
1781 by the British astronomer William
Herschel. Uranus orbits the Sun on its
side. This tipped rotational axis gives
rise to extreme seasons on Uranus. It is
thought that its unusual spin is due to a
collision with another planet-sized object
millions of years ago.

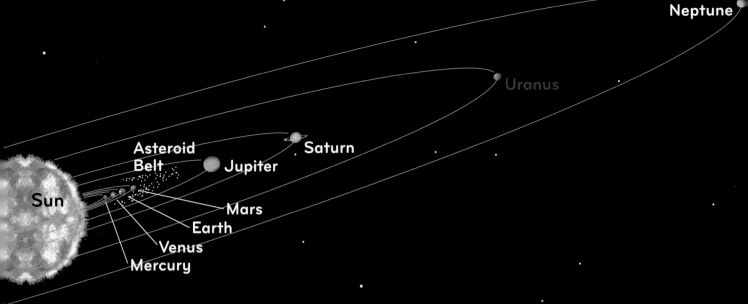

Neptune

Uranus

Saturn

Asteroid
Belt

Jupiter

Sun

Mars

Earth

Venus

Mercury

This 2006 image taken by the *Hubble Space Telescope* shows bands and a dark spot in Uranus's atmosphere

Earth in comparison

Uranus Facts

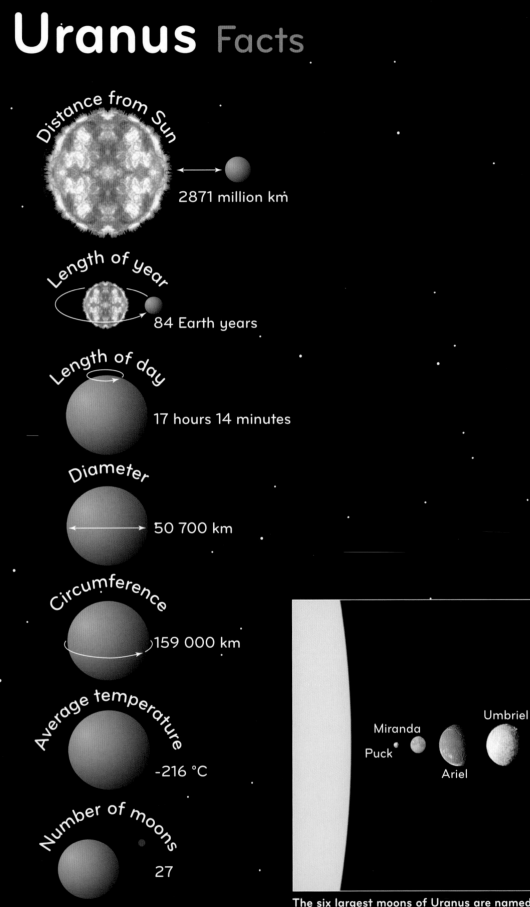

Distance from Sun

2871 million km

Length of year

84 Earth years

Length of day

17 hours 14 minutes

Diameter

50 700 km

Circumference

159 000 km

Average temperature

-216 °C

Number of moons

27

Miranda

Puck

Ariel

Umbriel

Titania

Oberon

The six largest moons of Uranus are named after characters from the works of William Shakespeare and Alexander Pope

The extreme seasons on Uranus

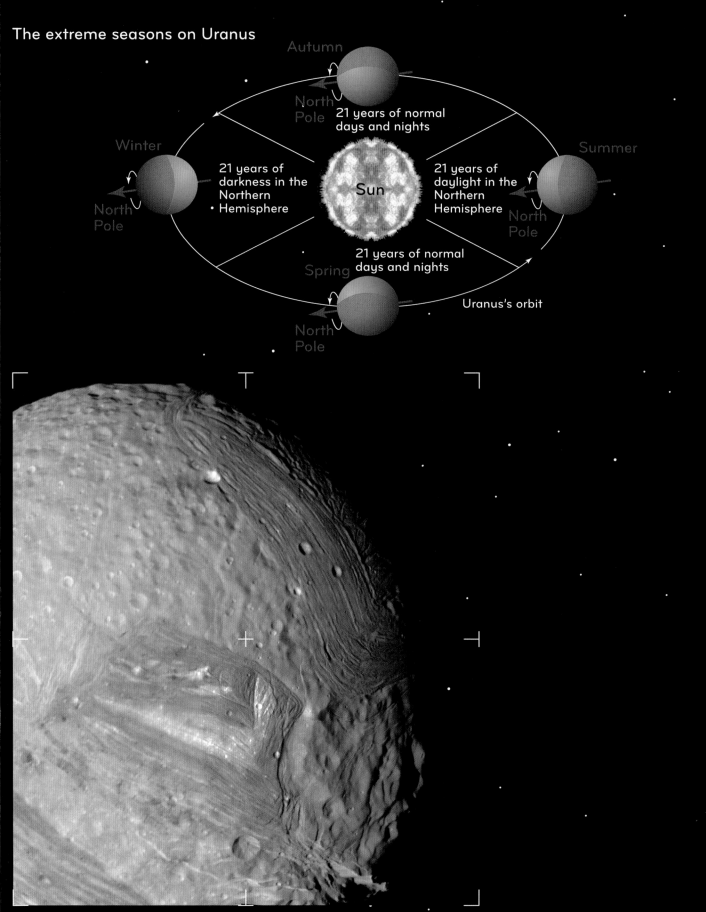

Autumn

North Pole

21 years of normal days and nights

Winter

North Pole

21 years of darkness in the Northern Hemisphere

Sun

21 years of daylight in the Northern Hemisphere

Summer

North Pole

21 years of normal days and nights

Spring

North Pole

Uranus's orbit

This image of the surface of Miranda displays many different geological features

Neptune
The furthest planet

Named after the Roman god of the sea, probably because of its deep blue colour, Neptune is also the windiest planet in the Solar System. It spins once every sixteen hours. Orbiting Neptune are at least thirteen moons and a ring system. Several dark spots have been seen on Neptune. The largest is about the size of Earth and is known as the Great Dark Spot. It may be a huge storm like the Great Red Spot on Jupiter. In the 1990s the spot vanished and another appeared in a new location.

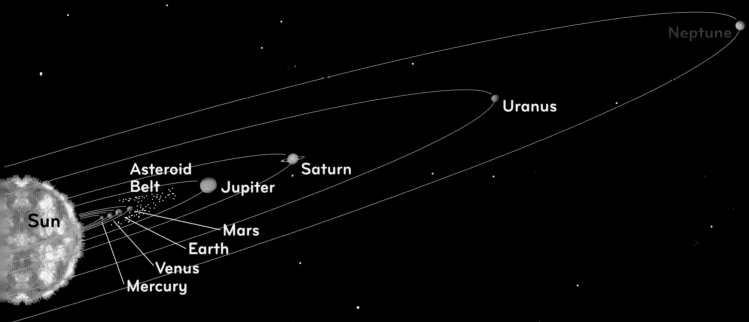

Neptune

Uranus

Saturn

Jupiter

Asteroid Belt

Mars

Earth

Venus

Mercury

Sun

Neptune is the last of the Gas Giants in the
Solar System and is more than thirty times
as far from the Sun as Earth

Earth in comparison

Neptune Facts

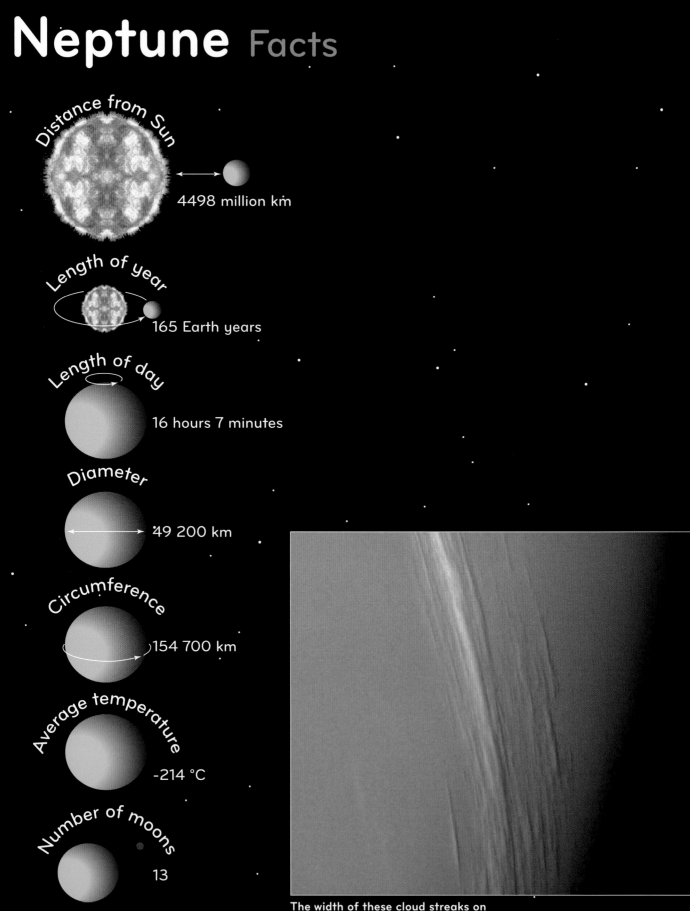

Distance from Sun
4498 million km

Length of year
165 Earth years

Length of day
16 hours 7 minutes

Diameter
49 200 km

Circumference
154 700 km

Average temperature
-214 °C

Number of moons
13

The width of these cloud streaks on
Neptune range from 50 to 200 km

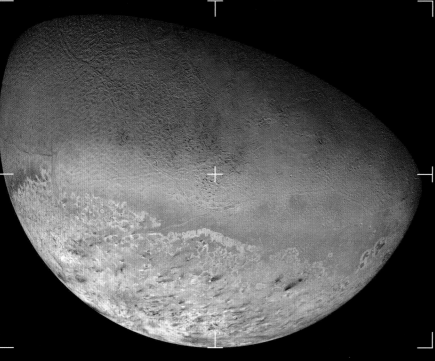

Triton, Neptune's largest moon, is one of the coldest objects in the Solar System, with a surface temperature of about −235 °C

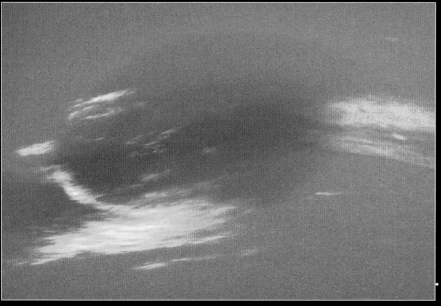

The winds near the Great Dark Spot on Neptune have been measured to be about 2400 km per hour

Neptune is thirty times the distance away from the Sun than Earth

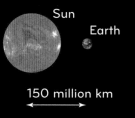

Sun

Earth

Neptune

150 million km

4498 million km

Pluto
The dwarf planet

Pluto was discovered in 1930. For a long time it was thought to be the ninth and furthest planet from the Sun. In 2006 it was reclassified as a dwarf planet. Pluto has four moons orbiting it. Charon, the largest, was discovered in 1978 and is almost as large as Pluto. The two objects appear to spin around each other, taking six days to complete a full orbit. Photographs of Pluto suggest that it has a surface of frozen gas and may have a thin atmosphere.

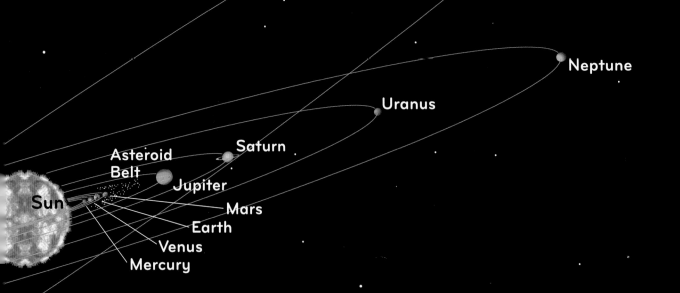

Pluto

Neptune

Uranus

Saturn

Asteroid
Belt

Jupiter

Mars

Earth

Venus

Sun

Mercury

Pluto is so small and distant that the task
of seeing the surface is as challenging as trying
to see the markings on a football 40 miles away.

Pluto and Earth compared

Pluto Facts

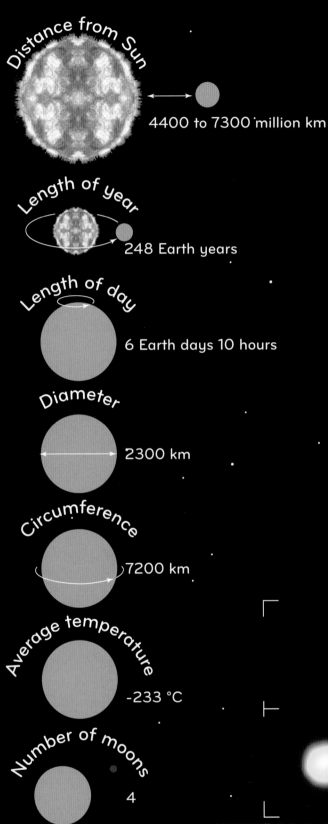

Distance from Sun

4400 to 7300 million km

Length of year

248 Earth years

Length of day

6 Earth days 10 hours

Diameter

2300 km

Circumference

7200 km

Average temperature

-233 °C

Number of moons

4

The distance between Pluto and its largest moon Charon is only 20 000 km

Pluto superimposed on a map of the United States of America

Pluto's orbit is so eccentric there are times
when it is closer to the Sun than Neptune

Comets

Comets are balls of rock and dirty ice that grow tails as they approach the Sun. They have oval shaped orbits and only come near to the Sun for a very short time. The solid part, the nucleus, of a comet is surrounded by glowing gases, the coma, which stretches out into a tail. Some comets have more than one tail, a bluish one which trails behind the comet and a yellowish one which follows the path of the comets orbit. Bright comets can only be seen from Earth once every ten years and those with long orbits may only be seen every few thousand years.

Parts of a comet

The tail of a comet, which always points away from the Sun, can become millions of kilometres long and make a wonderful sight

The coma is a cloud of glowing gases that surrounds the nucleus

The nucleus is made of ice mixed with rock, dust and grit

A comet's orbit around the Sun

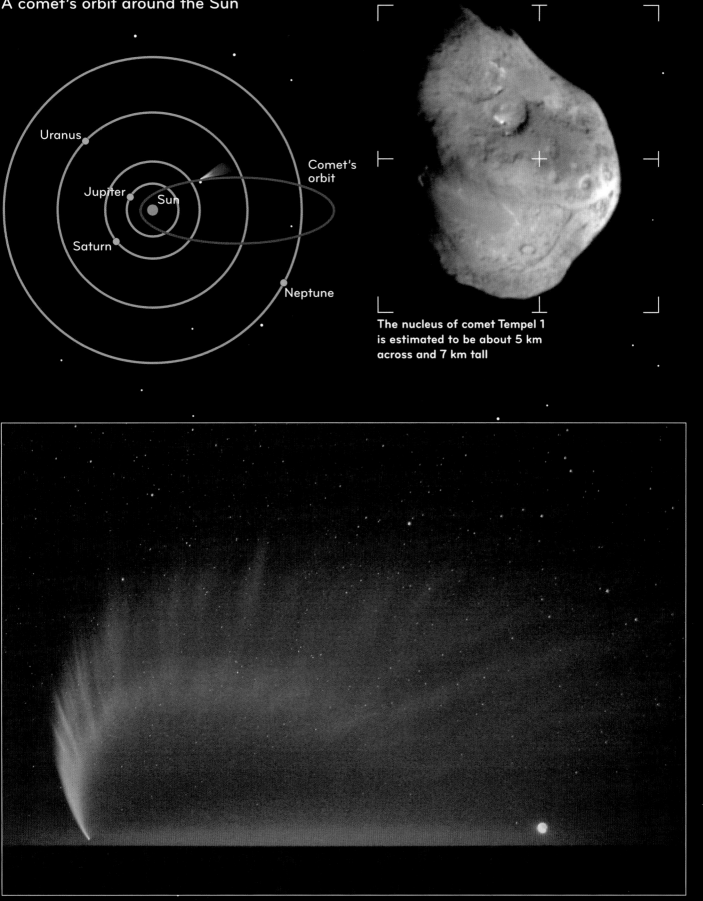

Uranus

Jupiter

Sun

Saturn

Neptune

Comet's orbit

The nucleus of comet Tempel 1 is estimated to be about 5 km across and 7 km tall

Comet McNaught and the setting sun over the Pacific Ocean on 1 January, 2007

Man and space

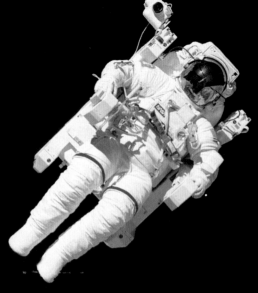

Sputnik 1

An astronaut leaves his spaceship

1957	The first artificial satellite, *Sputnik 1*, launched
1959	First photograph of Earth from orbit
1961	First man in space
1963	First woman in space
1965	First space walk
1966	First spacecraft to land on the Moon
1969	Man lands on the Moon

1980	*Voyager 1* passes Saturn
1981	First Space Shuttle launch
1986	Space Shuttle *Challenger* disaster
1986	*Voyager 2* passes Uranus
1989	*Voyager 2* passes Neptune

1957 – 1969   **1970 – 1979**   **1980 – 1989**

1970	First lunar rover
1971	First space station
1972	Last man on the moon
1975	First images of Venus
1976	First images of Mars
1977	Voyager spacecrafts launched
1979	First images of Jupiter and Saturn

Mars Exploration Rover

Lunar Module on the Moon's surface

Hubble Space
Telescope

Space Shuttle

United States

2000 First orbit of an asteroid
2001 First landing on an asteroid
2001 First tourist in space
2004 First Mars rover
2004 First orbit of Saturn
2011 Final Space Shuttle launch

1990 – 1999   2000 – Present

1990 *Magellan* arrives at
Venus
1990 *Hubble Space Telescope*
launched
1991 First asteroid flyby
1995 First orbit of Jupiter
1998 First module of
*International Space
Station* launched

Apollo 11 blasts-off
to take man to the
Moon in 1969

Voyager 2

Solar System at a glance

Name	Diameter	Circumference	Distance from Sun	Average temperature
Sun	1 391 016 km	4 370 000 km	...	5504 °C
Mercury	4900 km	15 300 km	58 million km	-173 °C to 427 °C
Venus	12 100 km	38 000 km	108 million km	462 °C
Earth	12 700 km	40 000 km	150 million km	15 °C
Mars	6779 km	21 300 km	228 million km	-63 °C
Jupiter	143 000 km	450 000 km	778 million km	-148 °C
Saturn	116 500 km	366 000 km	1427 million km	-178 °C
Uranus	50 700 km	159 000 km	2871 million km	-216 °C
Neptune	49 200 km	154 700 km	4498 million km	-214 °C
Pluto	2300 km	7 200 km	4400 to 7300 million km	-233 °C

Length of year	Length of day	Number of moons	Symbol
...	25 Earth days 9 hours		☉
88 Earth days	59 Earth days	none	☿
224 Earth days 17 hours	243 Earth days	none	♀
365 days 6 hours	23 hours 56 mins	1	⊕
687 Earth days	24 hours 37 mins	2	♂
11 Earth years 314 days	9 hours 55 mins	63	♃
29 Earth years	10 hours 39 mins	62	♄
84 Earth years	17 hours 14 mins	27	♅
165 Earth years	16 hours 7 mins	13	♆
248 Earth years	6 Earth days 10 hours	4	♇

Quiz 1

1 The Solar System includes

- 5 planets
- 10 planets
- 8 planets
- 12 planets

2 Which planet has the shortest orbit?

- Earth
- Mercury
- Venus
- Neptune

3 Which planet in the Solar System has rings?

- Saturn
- Uranus
- Neptune
- All of the above

Answers at the back of the book

4 Which planet is furthest
   from the Sun?

   ● Earth
   ● Neptune
   ● Saturn
   ● Mars

5 How many moons does
   Mars have?

   ● 3
   ● 2
   ● 63
   ● 27

6 How long does it take for
   Earth to orbit the Sun?

   ● 365 days 6 hours
   ● 165 years
   ● 88 days
   ● 84 years

Quiz 2

1 Which planet can support life?

- Neptune
- Venus
- Earth
- All of the above

2 Which planet is nearest the Sun?

- Neptune
- Mars
- Earth
- Mercury

3 Which planet is made up mostly of gases?

- Mercury
- Earth
- Jupiter
- Venus

74

4 Which planet is referred to as the Red Planet?

- Venus
- Mars
- Earth
- Uranus

5 Which is the largest planet in the Solar System?

- Earth
- Mercury
- Venus
- Jupiter

6 Which planet is named after the Roman goddess of love?

- Venus
- Saturn
- Earth
- Jupiter

Answers at the back of the book

Glossary

anti-clockwise	The direction that the majority of the objects move in our Solar System.
asteroid	An object made up of rocks and metal, that orbits a star and is found in space.
astronomer	Someone who studies space, including the planets, stars, galaxies, comets and astronomy.
atmosphere	The layer of gases surrounding the surface of a planet, moon or star.
circumference	A measurement taken around the fattest, middle part of a planet.
comet	Small ball of dirty ice, dust and gas which orbits the Sun (often in oval orbits). Comets are only visible from Earth when they are close enough to the Sun to start burning off their dust/gas. Some comets take a few decades to complete an orbit, others take thousands of years. Some comets are also known to orbit Jupiter.
core	The centre of a space object, such as a planet, moon, or star.
crater	A bowl-shaped depression on the surface of a planet, moon or asteroid formed when a meteorite or another asteroid hits the surface.
crust	The thin rocky outer surface of a planet or moon.
day	Length of time it takes for a planet to completely rotate on its axis.
dwarf planet	A rounded body orbiting the Sun. Pluto, Ceres and Eris are examples of dwarf planets.
equator	An imaginery line running around the middle of a planet.
galaxy	A large group of stars, bound together by gravity.
Gas Giant	A type of planet with small, dense cores that do not have a solid surface, rather they are made of of gas and liquids. Examples include Jupiter, Saturn, Uranus and Neptune.
gravity	The force that pulls our Universe together.
inner planets	Those planets closest to the Sun, known as Mercury, Venus, Earth and Mars.
lava flow	Refers to moving molten rock expelled from a volcano. Only Earth and Io (a moon of Jupiter) currently have active volcanoes in our Solar System.
mantle	The area surrounding the core of a rocky planet.
Milky Way	The spiral galaxy, containing over 100 billion stars creating a broad band of light in the night sky, in which our Solar System is located.

moon	Any mini-planet which orbits another planet.
orbit	The path of one object as it revolves around another object. For example, the planets orbit, or travel around the Sun.
outer planets	Those planets in our Solar System, furthest from the Sun, beyond the asteroid belt, which includes Jupiter, Saturn, Uranus and Neptune.
planet	A large object or ball made up of rock or gas, which orbits a star and has a solid core. There are eight planets in our Solar System.
planetoid	Another term for asteroids, which are also called mini-planets.
plates	The Earth's solid surface is broken up into moving pieces or plates. It is the only planet in the Solar System to have active plates.
pole	Planets have two poles, which are the furthest points away from its equator.
rotate	Planets spin around their central axis. Earth rotates about its axis every 24 hours.
satellite	Any object in outer space that goes around another object. For example, the Moon is a satellite of Earth or man-made satellites orbit the Earth.
solar	The latin term 'Sol' translates to Sun, so solar refers to anything related to the Sun.
Solar System	The group of eight planets, and other objects, such as moons, ice and rocks, that all orbit around the Sun.
spiral galaxy	A galaxy often forms a circular shape, whereby the stars, gas and dust are gathered in long spiral arms winding outward from the galaxy's centre.
star	A ball of exploding gas held together by its own gravity.
Sun	A medium-sized yellow star at the centre of our Solar System, with a diameter 100 times that of Earth.
tail	A tail or a coma is the visible dust and gas that melts off a comet as it passes by the Sun. It is blown away from the Sun by the solar winds.
terrestrial planet	Planets mostly made up of rock, such as the four planets of the inner Solar System (Mercury, Venus, Earth, and Mars).
year	The length of time it takes a planet to go around the Sun. Earth's year lasts 365 days 6 hours.

Index

Quiz answers

Quiz 1 (page 72)

1	8 planets	4	Neptune
2	Mercury	5	2
3	All of the above	6	365 days 6 hours

Quiz 2 (page 74)

1	Earth	4	Mars
2	Mercury	5	Jupiter
3	Jupiter	6	Venus